SKIING
EXERCISES

EXERCISES FOR BEGINNERS AND INTERMEDIATE SKIERS

All forms of exercise may pose some risks, and before beginning any exercise or training programme, consult your physician.

Professional's insights: Simon Tasch
Editor: Agnes Przybylska
Photos: Andrew Pesheck
Layout: landie.pl
ISBN: 978-83-63017-92-7
Several of our publications may be purchased on: www.sport-book.co
We hope you enjoy our sites.

LIST OF CONTENTS

PEOPLE INVOLVED IN MAKING OF THIS BOOK:

Simon Tasch
AUTHOR: EXERCISES

Mountains, for skiing and for many years equally for cycling, are the love of my life. I have skied since early childhood and for several years have been one of the leading Polish alpinists and with the national team. For some time now I have specialised in the free riding, that is extreme riding off the track.

For almost 20 years now I have also practised high-performance cycling and Down Hill MTB where I was the Champion of Poland in the „masters".

Andrew Pesheck
BOOK DESIGN AND PICTURES

Sports and photography are what makes me tick. The obvious link is the sports photography. In winter I go skiing, in summer I go jogging, swimming and diving, and everywhere I go I take my photographer's backpack - its extra weight is a small price to pay. You will find more about me on www.andrzejpeszek.pl.

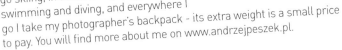

WHO THE "SKI EXCERCISES..." ARE DEDICATED TO

The answer to the above question is simple: to all who love skiing and wish to ski better.

Most of you are self-taught skiers, at least in a substantial part of your skiing careers. Of course, intensive lessons on the slopes with a good instructor will bring the best results, but due to financial or other reasons not everyone may take advantage of them. Even if you have a chance to periodically ski with an instructor, you will not ski with one forever, and sooner or later you will move on to a stage of self-improvement.

And then your self-reflection - e.g. when comparing pictures or films of your skiing with the technique of "masters" observed on the slopes or when listening to kind advice of your friends - will often allow you to notice you do weird things with your arms, or your hips are in a rather awkward position.

A diagnosis is only half the battle to correct some errors, the other half is proper exercises and this is what our book is about. It is a book worth returning to, even if you do not have any objections (nor does anyone else) to your skiing technique. The enclosed exercises will allow you to strengthen your good habits, to recall the key elements of the ski technique at the beginning of a ski season, or most desirably, at the beginning of each day.

INTRO

TERMS USED IN THE BOOK:

In the book, as usual in all somewhat specialist publications, we use a specialist language - a sort of "skier dialect". To avoid confusion, let's explain each term.

- centre (inside) of a turn/turn centre:
a place, area, direction to the centre of an arc (circle) through which your skis move

- outside (outer side) of a turn:
a place, area, direction on the outer side of an arc (circle) through which your skis move

- inside/uphill ski, leg, knee, hip, shoulder, arm, hand or pole:
located to the centre (inside) of a turn

- outside/downhill ski, leg, knee, hip, shoulder, arm, hand or pole:
located on the outside of a turn

-weighting of the outside/inside ski:
shifting the greater part (and sometimes all) of your weight to one of the skis

-weighting ski tips/tails:
shifting the greater part of your weight to a given part of the skis

-hips/knees angulation:
‚breaking' the silhouette in hips/knees, causing a shifting of weight to the outside of a turn

-torso/shoulder counter-rotation:
twisting shoulders to the side (outside) of the direction in which your skis move

As a reminder to the more complex technical elements of skiing, we would like to invite you to read our books (see www.sport-book.co).

WARM UP

A warm up is probably the most neglected topic in the theory of skiing, and especially in practice; at the same time it has a significant impact on your skiing and especially on the risk of an injury. During the warm-up you "wake" your body up, you warm muscles by increasing the blood flow in them, increase a range of motion in the joints and what's very important you stimulate the so-called proprioceptors - i.e. deep sensory receptors - thanks to them you may control the degree of stretching of muscles, tendons and ligaments, as well as the alignment of different body parts while skiing; in other words all the nuances making up an excellent skiing technique.

So let's warm up...

**TORSO TWISTS
(10 TO 30 REPS)**

In the first exercise, use a pole held wide apart in a horizontal position and make wide arcs, twisting torso as much as possible. Starting with gentler twists, gradually increase their depth with each repetition until you come to the maximum back twist (for your body build). Perform full repetitions starting with a complete twist to the right followed by a full left twist.

MOVING SKI POLE BEHIND YOUR BACK (10 TO 30 REPS)

Holding a pole with arms wide apart, place it behind a shoulder joint. This exercise requires a fairly good flexibility of the shoulder joints. If you have problems with doing this exercise, you may practice swinging your arms back in a similar fashion, i.e. to exercise with a "virtual pole". Exercise the right and left side in turns.

WARM UP

HIP ROTATIONS
(10 TO 30 REPS IN EACH DIRECTION)

Standing at ease (with feet slightly wider apart than the hip width) place hands on the hips and perform wide hip rotations. Rotate around clockwise 5 to 10 times and then repeat it anticlockwise.

TORSO ROTATIONS
(10 TO 30 REPS IN EACH DIRECTION)

Standing with legs fairly wide apart, perform extensive torso rotations: during the downward move hands touch the snow, and in the upward move you slightly bend back. Perform 2–5 repetitions in one direction and then change the direction.

>WARM U

FORWARD AND BACKWARD LEG SWINGS
(EACH LEG 10 TO 30 REPS)

Standing on one leg and leaning on poles, perform extensive forward and backward swings with the other leg. If possible, the torso remains still. Perform 5 to 10 swings with one leg and then change legs.

SIDE LEG SWINGS
(EACH LEG 10 TO 30 REPS)

Standing on one leg and leaning on poles, perform extensive side leg swings with the other leg. If possible, the torso remains still. During the side move a leg reaches the right angle or even passes the horizontal line and in the back move it crosses the central line to perform a downswing preparing for another backswing. Perform 5 to 10 swings with one leg and then change legs.

WARM U

KNEE ROTATIONS (PARALLEL)
(10 TO 20 REPS IN EACH DIRECTION)

Standing with your feet at hip width and your hands on the knees, perform knee rotations. Try to make the move as extensive as possible, especially to the sides (but don't exaggerate). Perform 2 to 5 repetitions to one side and then change directions.

Standing with feet slightly wider than hip width and with hands on the knees, perform symmetric knee rotations (knees do not rotate "together" like in the previous exercise, but in turn move towards and away from each other). Try to make the move as extensive as possible (but don't exaggerate). Perform 2 to 5 repetitions in one directions (e.g. rotating forward inside) and then change directions (rotating forward outwards).

>WARM U

SIDE LUNGE STRETCH
(10-30 REPS ON EACH SIDE)

Standing with legs wide astride to the side, rhythmically deepen the lunge by raising and lowering of the hips.

FRONT LUNGE STRETCH
(3 TO 10 LUNGES ON EACH LEG)

Leaning on poles, make a deep front lunge, and then deepen it 2 to 5 times rhythmically raising and lowering the hips.

andie.pl
Health and Leisure

PROPER SKIING SILHOUETTE

This group of exercises will cover the following basic elements of the technique that make up the correct ski silhouette:

• overall balance (side-to-side and front-to-back)

• correct breaking of the silhouette with knees and hips angulation to the centre of a turn

• weighting of the outside ski and ski tips

• up-and-down motion

PROPER SKIING
SILHOUETTE

AIM:

○ side-to-side/lateral balance

○ fore/aft balance

○ feeling the edge-hold

LEVEL OF DIFFICULTY:

SKIING ON ONE SKI WITHOUT POLES

AIM:

- side-to-side/lateral balance
- fore/aft balance
- feeling the edge-hold

LEVEL OF DIFFICULTY:

☆☆☆☆☆

Stand facing directly across a slope. Put on only one ski, and practicing without poles, perform movements imitating driving on a scooter. Push with your free leg and try to cover as much distance on the ski as possible; before losing the momentum push off once again. Practice skiing on both the

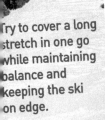

Try to cover a long stretch in one go while maintaining balance and keeping the ski on edge.

outside edge (skiing on the uphill ski) and the inside edge (on the downhill ski).

If performing the exercise without poles is a problem, you may begin with the version with the poles – "scooter for beginners".

Please pay attention to: keeping balance and edging a ski.

PROPER SKIING SILHOUETTE

SNOW-PLOUGH ARCS WITH POLES HELD DIAGONALLY IN FRONT

AIM:

- weighting of the outside ski
- knee angulation
- hip angulation

LEVEL OF DIFFICULTY:

☆☆☆☆☆

SNOW-PLOUGH ARCS WITH POLES HELD DIAGONALLY IN FRONT

Poles you hold are visibly diagonal, the lower end touches the knee of the outside leg.

While skiing in snow-plough position, perform a turn into the slope while holding poles diagonally in the front (the lower end of poles touches the knee of the outside leg). This positioning of poles forces breaking the silhouette in the knees and hips – "knee and

AIM:

- weighting of the outside ski
- knee angulation
- hip angulation

LEVEL OF DIFFICULTY:

☆☆☆☆☆

hip angulation" and weighting of the outside ski. Ski until you come to a complete stop (at this moment skis are pointed slightly uphill), turn around and perform an arc to the other side. Once you master this version of the exercise, you may move on to the version of the combined snow-plough arcs switching smoothly from one to the next turn without stopping.

Please pay attention to: pronounced breaking of the silhouette in the hips.

> PROPER SKIING
SILHOUETTE

ANDRZEJ█PESZEK
PHOTOGRAPHY

SNOW-PLOUGH SKIING "FOLK DANCE" STYLE

AIM:

- hip angulation
- torso counter-rotation
- weighting the tips

LEVEL OF DIFFICULTY:

☆☆☆☆☆

PROPER SKIING SILHOUETTE

SNOW-PLOUGH SKIING "FOLK DANCE" STYLE

AIM:

- hip angulation
- torso counter-rotation
- weighting the tips

LEVEL OF DIFFICULTY:

☆☆☆☆☆

Ehili skiing in snow-plough position put the outside hand on the outside hip and raise the inside arm to the front. The hand on the hip "actively" pushes the hip to the inside of a turn; the extended inside arm maintains the body in a more or less counter-rotation position to the

The raised arm in front of the torso forces counter-rotation.

direction of skiing (shoulder line is not aligned perfectly perpendicular to the direction of skiing, it is slightly twisted to the outside of a turn). Upon reaching the traverse, change hands and move the centre of gravity to the other side by switching the edges.

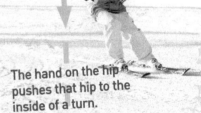

The hand on the hip pushes that hip to the inside of a turn.

Please pay attention to: "active" pushing out of a hip.

> PROPER SKIING
SILHOUETTE

„FOLK DANCE"

AIM:

- hip angulation
- torso counter-rotation
- weighting the tips

LEVEL OF DIFFICULTY:

> PROPER SKIING
SILHOUETTE

„FOLK DANCE"

Change hands during transition phase.

AIM:

- hip angulation
- torso counter-rotation
- weighting the tips

LEVEL OF DIFFICULTY:

☆☆☆☆☆

Making shorter or longer-radius turns, put the outside hand on the outside hip (pushing it into the centre of a turn) and raise the other arm forward (forcing counter-rotation of the torso and weighting of the ski tips).

Please pay attention to: "active" pushing out of a hip

> PROPER SKIING
SILHOUETTE

SNOW-PLOUGH SKIING WITH OUTSIDE HAND ON KNEE OF OUTSIDE LEG

AIM:

- weighting of the outside ski
- knee angulation
- hip angulation

LEVEL OF DIFFICULTY:

★★★★★

SNOW-PLOUGH SKIING WITH OUTSIDE HAND ON KNEE OF OUTSIDE LEG

AIM:

- weighting of the outside ski
- knee angulation
- hip angulation

The hand on the knee helps in knee and hip angulation to the centre of the turn, while the other arm helps to twist shoulders slightly to the outside of the turn.

LEVEL OF DIFFICULTY:

☆☆☆☆☆

While snow-ploughing, put the outside hand on the knee of the outside leg (slightly pushing the knee to the centre of a turn). This position ensures breaking the silhouette in the hips and knees. The other arm is raised forward, what in turn forces counter-rotation of the torso/shoulders.

Please pay attention to: "active" pushing of a knee to the centre of a turn.

PROPER SKIING
SILHOUETTE

SKIING WITH HANDS PLACED ON KNEES

AIM:

- weighting the tips
- low silhouette

LEVEL OF DIFFICULTY:

☆☆☆☆☆

SKIING WITH HANDS PLACED ON KNEES

AIM:

- weighting the tips
- low silhouette

LEVEL OF DIFFICULTY:

☆☆☆☆☆

Making longer or shorter-radius turns (start with long-radius turns and gradually after gaining practice move to exercises with shorter-radius turns), place your hands on the knees. In this position, actively press against your knees (and in effect on the skis) to the front and angulate them to the centre of successive turns.

Putting hands on your knees helps to properly press the legs and skis, and additionally forces a low silhouette.

Please pay attention to: "active" pushing of the knees to the front and centre of a turn.

> PROPER SKIING
SILHOUETTE

> PROPER SKIING
> SILHOUETTE

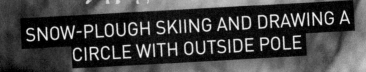

SNOW-PLOUGH SKIING AND DRAWING A CIRCLE WITH OUTSIDE POLE

AIM:

- weighting of the outside ski
- hip angulation

LEVEL OF DIFFICULTY:

☆☆☆☆☆

>PROPER SKIING SILHOUETTE

SNOW-PLOUGH SKIING AND DRAWING A CIRCLE WITH OUTSIDE POLE

AIM:

- weighting of the outside ski
- hip angulation

LEVEL OF DIFFICULTY:

☆☆☆☆☆

While snow-ploughing, "draw" a circle to the outside of a turn.

Snow-plough with one pole held in the outside hand and "draw" a circle on the outside of a turn. Try to reach as far as you can - this position ensures the hip angulation to the centre of a turn, shifting of the centre of gravity to the outside ski and weighting of this ski. In the transition phase move the pole to the other hand and perform the exercise in the other direction.

Please pay attention to: drawing wide circles.

PROPER SKIING SILHOUETTE

PROPER SKIING
SILHOUETTE

ABSORBING BUMPS

AIM:

- up-and-down motion
- calm upper body
- overall balance

LEVEL OF DIFFICULTY:

ABSORBING BUMPS

AIM:

- up-and-down motion
- calm upper body
- overall balance

LEVEL OF DIFFICULTY:

☆☆☆☆☆

You need to find a "bump" on a trail (start with smaller mounds and as you gain practice, move on to higher humps). Skiing long-radius turns (not in a straight line as with the current waisted skis which when put flat tend to catch at the edges and "pull") ride onto a bump lowering your

silhouette and ski down the bump gradually straightening up. Your upper body should remain on the same level at all times, while bumps are absorbed with the bending of knees and of torso at the waist (if it is necessary due to the mogul's height).

Please pay attention to: bending legs and torso at the waist during riding over and straightening when skiing off a bump.

> PROPER SKIING
SILHOUETTE

Majesty

TRULY INDEPENDENT FREESKI COMPANY

Majesty Ace

MAJESTYSKIS.COM
rider: Szymon Styrczula Maśniak., photo: Marcin Kin

SQUATING DOWN

AIM:

- up-and-down motion
- równowaga przód-tył

LEVEL OF DIFFICULTY:

★★★★★

PROPER SKIING
SILHOUETTE

SQUATING DOWN

AIM:

- up-and-down motion
- fore/aft balance

LEVEL OF DIFFICULTY:

☆☆☆☆☆

Please pay attention to: fluidity, slow and controlled upward and downward movements.

Making a long-radius turn (almost in a straight line) with poles on your shoulders, gradually lower your silhouette, going down as low as possible and then slowly and fluently straighten the silhouette up. As you gain experience, perform this exercise at increasingly higher speeds and on steeper slopes.

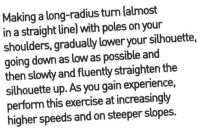

Go down as low as you can, then remain in this position a moment and rise slowly.

PROPER SKIING SILHOUETTE

PREPARING FOR SHORT TURNS

Short turns (Wedeln) - a basic ski technique - above all require good up-and-down dynamics, proper coordination of the upper body, but most of all - ski poles and active lower body (legs) and a silhouette pointing downhill.

UPWARD MOVEMENT WITH POLE PLANTING

AIM:

- up-and-down motion
- fore/aft balance
- synchronisation of upper and lower body movements

LEVEL OF DIFFICULTY:

☆☆☆☆☆

UPWARD MOVEMENT WITH POLE PLANTING

AIM:

- up-and-down motion
- fore/aft balance
- synchronisation of upper and lower body movements

LEVEL OF DIFFICULTY:

☆☆☆☆☆

While traversing, crouch in a low-silhouette position and then make a quite rapid upward motion and plant a pole at the same time. The process of pole "planting" begins when you are still in a low position (with flexing of your wrist to direct the pole's tip into place where you will plant it) and ends (with the pole dug down vertically), when you are in a fully upright position.

Beginning with low-silhouette position, make an upward motion while thrusting a pole.

Please pay attention to: proper coordination of straightening the body and pole planting.

PREPARING FOR SHORT TURNS

"FOLK DANCE" WITH A CLAP

AIM:

- L-H sequence
- hip angulation

LEVEL OF DIFFICULTY:

☆☆☆☆☆

PREPARING
SHORT TURN

„FOLK DANCE" WITH A CLAP

AIM:

- L-H sequence
- hip angulation

LEVEL OF DIFFICULTY:

☆☆☆☆☆

Making a relatively long-radius turn (and once you become more confident, increasingly shorter turns), put the outside hand on the outside hip, "pushing" the hip to the inside of a turn ("folk dance" position). During the transition phase make an upward motion and clap hands over your head. This movement ensures execution of the L-H (low-high) sequence and unweighting of skis in the transition phase.

Please pay attention to: correct "folk dance" position and high claps during the transition phase.

At the time of transition clap hands over your head.

> PREPARING FOR SHORT TURNS

HOLDING KNEES - UPWARD MOVEMENT - CLAPING HANDS DURING SHORT TURNS (WEDELN)

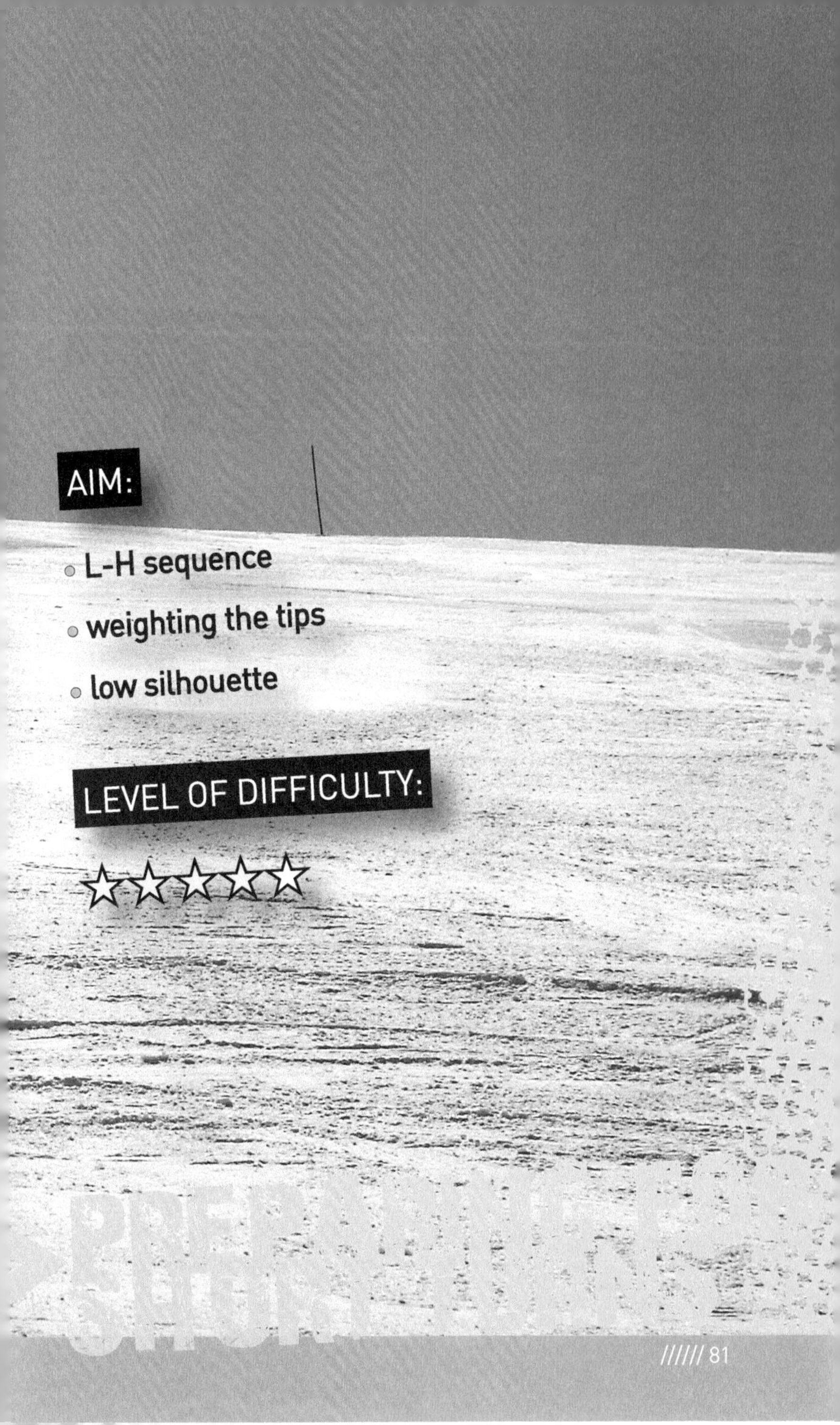

AIM:

- L-H sequence
- weighting the tips
- low silhouette

LEVEL OF DIFFICULTY:

☆☆☆☆☆

HOLDING KNEES - UPWARD MOVEMENT - CLAPING HANDS DURING SHORT TURNS (WEDELN)

AIM:

- L-H sequence
- weighting the tips
- low silhouette

LEVEL OF DIFFICULTY:

☆☆☆☆☆

Skiing short turns (Wedeln), put hands on the knees (correspondingly weighting ski tips and angulating knees to the centre of a turn). During the transition phase make an upward motion and clap hands over your head. This set of moves ensures a dynamic (from very low to very high silhouette) execution of the L-H sequence.

Please pay attention to: "active" knee weighting with hands and a high clap in the transition phase.

During a turn press your knees with your hands, weighting ski tips and angulating knees to the centre of a turn.

>PREPARING FOR SHORT TURNS

SHORT TURN (WEDELN) SKIING WITH RAISED INSIDE ARM AND OUTSIDE HAND ON OUTSIDE KNEE

AIM:

- torso counter-rotation
- hip angulation
- knee angulation
- L-H sequence

LEVEL OF DIFFICULTY:

☆☆☆☆☆

SHORT TURN (WEDELN) SKIING WITH RAISED INSIDE ARM AND OUTSIDE HAND ON OUTSIDE KNEE

The hand on your knee pushes it to the centre of a turn; the raised arm ensures counter-rotation of torso/shoulders.

AIM:

- torso counter-rotation
- hip angulation
- knee angulation
- L-H sequence

LEVEL OF DIFFICULTY:

☆☆☆☆☆

Skiing short turns (Wedeln), put the outside hand on the outside knee (pushing it to the centre of a turn) and raise the other arm to the front, thus setting the shoulder line to point downhill. During the transition phase make an upward motion (L-H sequence) and change hands.

Please pay attention to: "active" weighting of a knee and an arm raised to the front.

> PREPARING FOR SHORT TURNS

INTRODUCTION TO CARVING

Carving : an excellent stance on the edge of the skis, breaking the silhouette (in the hips and knees) and calm upper body.

INTRODUCTION
TO CARVING

SHARP TURN INTO THE SLOPE

AIM:

- setting skis on the edges
- calm upper body
- shoulders perpendicular to skiing direction

LEVEL OF DIFFICULTY:

☆☆☆☆☆

Keep turning to
a complete stop.

SHARP TURN INTO THE SLOPE

AIM:

- setting skis on the edges
- calm upper body
- shoulders perpendicular to skiing direction

LEVEL OF DIFFICULTY:

☆☆☆☆☆

On a gently inclined slope, pronouncedly edge both of your skis and perform a smooth turn in to the slope until you come to a complete stop. Once you stop, turn about and perform the exercise to the other side. As you progress, choose steeper slopes; in time you may try to link the turns (of course, in such a situation they are no longer turns in to the slope).

Please pay attention to: pronounced edging of both skis.

INTRODUCTION TO CARVING

HOLDING KNEES - UPWARD MOVEMENT - A CLAP IN LONG-RADIUS TURN

AIM:

- L-H sequence
- weighting the tips
- low silhouette

LEVEL OF DIFFICULTY:

☆☆☆☆☆

HOLDING KNEES - UPWARD MOVEMENT - A CLAP IN LONG-RADIUS TURN

AIM:

- L-H sequence
- weighting the tips
- low silhouette

LEVEL OF DIFFICULTY:

☆☆☆☆☆

Please pay attention to: putting conscious pressure to the knees, and to a high clap.

Making a long-radius turn, put hands on your knees (weighting the ski tips and angulating knees to the centre of a turn) and in the transition phase, clap your hands once, high over your head.

During a turn press hands on your knees.

INTRODUCTION TO CARVING

SKIING WITH POLES IN RAISED INSIDE ARM

AIM:

- torso counter-rotation
- hip angulation
- weighting the tips
- calm upper body

LEVEL OF DIFFICULTY:

☆☆☆☆☆

SKIING WITH POLES IN RAISED INSIDE ARM

AIM:

- torso counter-rotation
- hip angulation
- weighting the tips
- calm upper body

Making a long-radius turn, raise your inside arm (with poles) to the front. This position reduces the tendency (if applicable) to excessive twisting of the torso after a turn and ensures counter-rotation of torso/shoulders. During the transition phase make an upward motion (L-H sequence) and change hands (switching the poles).

Please pay attention to: pronounced raising of the inside arm to the front.

INTRODUCTION TO CARVING

SKIING LONG-RADIUS TURNS WITH RAISED INSIDE ARM AND OUTSIDE HAND ON OUTSIDE KNEE

AIM:

- torso counter-rotation
- hip angulation
- knee angulation
- weighting the tips

LEVEL OF DIFFICULTY:

☆☆☆☆☆

INTRODUCTION TO CARVING

SKIING LONG-RADIUS TURNS WITH RAISED INSIDE ARM AND OUTSIDE HAND ON OUTSIDE KNEE

Please pay attention to: pronounced pressing against a knee and raising of the opposite arm.

AIM:

- torso counter-rotation
- hip angulation
- knee angulation
- weighting the tips

LEVEL OF DIFFICULTY:
☆☆☆☆☆

Making a long-radius turn, put your outside hand on the outside knee and raise the inside arm to the front. The hand on your knee helps weighting the ski fronts and angulates the knee to the centre of a turn; the other arm is raised to the front, ensuring shoulders' position in a partial counter-rotation. During the transition phase perform upward motion (L-H sequence) and change hands.

In a long-radius turn, one hand is pressed against a knee and the other arm raised to the front.

INTRODUCTION TO CARVING

SKIING LONG-RADIUS TURNS WITH SKIS TO THE SIDES, TOUCHING KNEE

AIM:

- torso counter-rotation
- low silhouette
- hip angulation
- L-H sequence

LEVEL OF DIFFICULTY:

☆☆☆☆☆

SKIING LONG-RADIUS TURNS WITH SKIS TO THE SIDES, TOUCHING KNEE

AIM:

- torso counter-rotation
- low silhouette
- hip angulation
- L-H sequence

Please pay attention to: pressing poles to the outside knee.

LEVEL OF DIFFICULTY:

☆☆☆☆☆

Making a long-radius turn, keep poles in both hands, to one side, parallel to the ground – touching the outer knee with them in the middle of their length. This ensures lowering of silhouette and breaking it the in the hips and knees. Poles are positioned diagonally, causing a tilting of your shoulders away from the direction of skiing (counter-rotation), preventing the fairly common tendency to over-rotate one's torso to the direction of a turn. During the transition phase follow the L-H sequence and switch the body's position.

Ski in long-radius turns with poles held to one side.

INTRODUCTION TO CARVING

SKIING WITH POLES TUCKED UNDER KNEES

AIM:

- shoulders perpendicular to skiing direction
- low silhouette
- performing smooth turns
- weighting the tips

LEVEL OF DIFFICULTY:

☆☆☆☆☆

SKIING WITH POLES TUCKED UNDER KNEES

AIM:

- shoulders perpendicular to skiing direction
- low silhouette
- performing smooth turns
- weighting the tips

LEVEL OF DIFFICULTY:

☆☆☆☆☆

Make a long-radius turn, tucking poles under your knees. This position ensures lowering of your silhouette and weighting of the ski fronts (with hands at the back you have to lean forward to keep balance). You have only a limited ability to change torso's position, therefore precise skiing on the edges becomes all the more important. In the transition phase make an upward motion (as far as you can) and change edges.

During the transition phase perform limited L-H sequence.

Please pay attention to: precise skiing on the edges.

INTRODUCTION TO CARVING

HOW TO EXERCISE ?

With pleasure, of course, but also in such a manner as to achieve desired effects (and this usually takes some discipline).

For starters, you might want to go through all the exercises, performing just one of them per each full slide (only in those places on a slope, of course, where it is possible). Next, you may either take a systematic approach (practicing all the exercises one by one, repeating the cycles on a regular basis) or take a selective approach (focusing on these elements of the technique and on corresponding exercises which give you the most problems). Observing others or the difficulty with which you perform an exercise may help you to assess, which elements of your technique may need to be improved (or, you may choose to analyse photos and films). When performing a given exercise, which usually serves several purposes, each time focus on one particular element and only after mastering of all individual elements, you may integrate them all into a single, well-executed exercise.

When you master all the exercises, you may create your own versions by combining their components (e.g. by adding hand claps or weighting of either knee with either hand) - a description of initial exercises will help you every time to set an appropriate goal.

You should begin each day of your skiing with one or several exercises (or even better, every "half" a day - i.e. in the morning and after a mid-day break), because muscle memory is not perfect and from time to time even experts should practice the basic elements of an excellent skiing technique.

HOW TO EXERCISE

BOOKS PUBLISHED BY LANDIE.PL

Landie.pl is the unique, dedicated to sport activities, publishing house.

We also recommend our other books:

SKIING ON ONE SKI WITHOUT POLES

Stand facing directly across a slope. Put on only one ski, and practicing without poles, perform movements imitating driving on a scooter. Push with your free leg and try to cover as much distance on the ski as possible; before losing the momentum push off once again. Practice skiing on both the outside edge (skiing on the uphill ski) and the inside edge (on the downhill ski).

If performing the exercise without poles is a problem, you may begin with the version with the poles – "scooter for beginners".
☆☆☆☆☆

AIM:
- side-to-side/lateral balance
- fore/aft balance
- feeling the edge-hold

SNOW-PLOUGH ARCS WITH POLES HELD DIAGONALLY IN FRONT

While skiing in snow-plough position, perform a turn into the slope while holding poles diagonally in the front (the lower end of poles touches the knee of the outside leg). This positioning of poles forces breaking the silhouette in the knees and hips – "knee and hip angulation" and weighting of the outside ski. Ski until you come to a complete stop (at this moment skis are pointed slightly uphill), turn around and perform an arc to the other side. Once you master this version of the exercise, you may move on to the version of the combined snow-plough arcs switching smoothly from one to the next turn without stopping.
☆☆☆☆☆

AIM:
- weighting of the outside ski
- knee angulation
- hip angulation

SNOW-PLOUGH SKIING "KRAKOWIAK" STYLE

Ehili skiing in snow-plough position put the outside hand on the outside hip and raise the inside arm to the front. The hand on the hip "actively" pushes the hip to the inside of a turn; the extended inside arm maintains the body in a more or less counter-rotation position to the direction of skiing (shoulder line is not aligned perfectly perpendicular to the direction of skiing, it is slightly twisted to the outside of a turn). Upon reaching the traverse, change hands and move the centre of gravity to the other side by switching the edges.

☆☆☆☆☆

AIM:
- **hip angulation**
- **torso counter-rotation**
- **weighting the tips**

„KRAKOWIAK"

Making shorter or longer-radius turns, put the outside hand on the outside hip (pushing it into the centre of a turn) and raise the other arm forward (forcing counter-rotation of the torso and weighting of the ski tips).

☆☆☆☆☆

AIM:
- **hip angulation**
- **torso counter-rotation**
- **weighting the tips**

SNOW-PLOUGH SKIING WITH OUTSIDE HAND ON KNEE OF OUTSIDE LEG

While snow-ploughing, put the outside hand on the knee of the outside leg (slightly pushing the knee to the centre of a turn). This position ensures breaking the silhouette in the hips and knees. The other arm is raised forward, what in turn forces counter-rotation of the torso/shoulders.

☆☆☆☆☆

AIM:
- **weighting of the outside ski**
- **knee angulation**
- **hip angulation**

SKIING WITH HANDS PLACED ON KNEES

Making longer or shorter-radius turns (start with long-radius turns and gradually after gaining practice move to exercises with shorter-radius turns), place your hands on the knees. In this position, actively press against your knees (and in effect on the skis) to the front and angulate them to the centre of successive turns.

☆☆☆☆☆

AIM:
- **weighting the tips**
- **low silhouette**

SNOW-PLOUGH SKIING AND DRAWING A CIRCLE WITH OUTSIDE POLE

Snow-plough with one pole held in the outside hand and "draw" a circle on the outside of a turn. Try to reach as far as you can - this position ensures the hip angulation to the centre of a turn, shifting of the centre of gravity to the outside ski and weighting of this ski. In the transition phase move the pole to the other hand and perform the exercise in the other direction.

☆☆☆☆☆

AIM:

○ **weighting of the outside ski**
○ **hip angulation**

ABSORBING BUMPS

You need to find a "bump" on a trail (start with smaller mounds and as you gain practice, move on to higher humps). Skiing long-radius turns (not in a straight line as with the current waisted skis which when put flat tend to catch at the edges and "pull") ride onto a bump lowering your silhouette and ski down the bump gradually straightening up. Your upper body should remain on the same level at all times, while bumps are absorbed with the bending of knees and of torso at the waist (if it is necessary due to the mogul's height).

☆☆☆☆☆

AIM:

○ **up-and-down motion**
○ **calm upper body**
○ **overall balance**

SQUATING DOWN

Making a long-radius turn (almost in a straight line) with poles on your shoulders, gradually lower your silhouette, going down as low as possible and then slowly and fluently straighten the silhouette up. As you gain experience, perform this exercise at increasingly higher speeds and on steeper slopes.

☆☆☆☆☆

AIM:
- **up-and-down motion**
- **fore/aft balance**

UPWARD MOVEMENT WITH POLE PLANTING

While traversing, crouch in a low-silhouette position and then make a quite rapid upward motion and plant a pole at the same time. The process of pole "planting" begins when you are still in a low position (with flexing of your wrist to direct the pole's tip into place where you will plant it) and ends (with the pole dug down vertically), when you are in a fully upright position.

☆☆☆☆☆

AIM:
- **up-and-down motion**
- **fore/aft balance**
- **synchronisation of upper and lower body movements**

"KRAKOWIAK" WITH A CLAP

Making a relatively long-radius turn
(and once you become more confident,
increasingly shorter turns), put the outside
hand on the outside hip, "pushing" the
hip to the inside of a turn ("Krakowiak"
position). During the transition phase
make an upward motion and clap
hands over your head. This movement
ensures execution of the L-H (low-high)
sequence and unweighting of skis in the
transition phase.

AIM:
- **L-H sequence**
- **hip angulation**

HOLDING KNEES - UPWARD MOVEMENT - CLAPING HANDS DURING SHORT TURNS (WEDELN)

Skiing short turns (Wedeln), put hands on
the knees (correspondingly weighting ski
tips and angulating knees to the centre
of a turn). During the transition phase
make an upward motion and clap hands
over your head. This set of moves ensures
a dynamic (from very low to very high
silhouette) execution of the L-H sequence.

AIM:
- **L-H sequence**
- **weighting the tips**
- **low silhouette**

SHORT TURN (WEDELN) SKIING WITH RAISED INSIDE ARM AND OUTSIDE HAND ON OUTSIDE KNEE

Skiing short turns (Wedeln), put the outside hand on the outside knee (pushing it to the centre of a turn) and raise the other arm to the front, thus setting the shoulder line to point downhill. During the transition phase make an upward motion (L-H sequence) and change hands.

☆☆☆☆☆

AIM:

- torso counter-rotation
- hip angulation
- knee angulation
- L-H sequence

SHARP TURN INTO THE SLOPE

On a gently inclined slope, pronouncedly edge both of your skis and perform a smooth turn in to the slope until you come to a complete stop. Once you stop, turn about and perform the exercise to the other side. As you progress, choose steeper slopes; in time you may try to link the turns (of course, in such a situation they are no longer turns in to the slope).

☆☆☆☆☆

AIM:

- setting skis on the edges
- calm upper body
- shoulders perpendicular to skiing direction

HOLDING KNEES - UPWARD MOVEMENT - A CLAP IN LONG-RADIUS TURN

Making a long-radius turn, put hands on your knees (weighting the ski tips and angulating knees to the centre of a turn) and in the transition phase, clap your hands once, high over your head.

☆☆☆☆☆

AIM:
- L-H sequence
- **weighting the tips**
- **low silhouette**

SKIING WITH POLES IN RAISED INSIDE ARM

Making a long-radius turn, raise your inside arm (with poles) to the front. This position reduces the tendency (if applicable) to excessive twisting of the torso after a turn and ensures counter-rotation of torso/shoulders. During the transition phase make an upward motion (L-H sequence) and change hands (switching the poles).

☆☆☆☆☆

AIM:
- **torso counter-rotation**
- **hip angulation**
- **weighting the tips**
- **calm upper body**

Making a long-radius turn, put your outside hand on the outside knee and raise the inside arm to the front. The hand on your knee helps weighting the ski fronts and angulates the knee to the centre of a turn; the other arm is raised to the front, ensuring shoulders' position in a partial counter-rotation. During the transition phase perform upward motion (L-H sequence) and change hands.

☆☆☆☆☆

AIM:

- torso counter-rotation
- hip angulation
- knee angulation
- weighting the tips

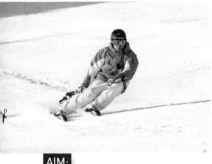

Making a long-radius turn, keep poles in both hands, to one side, parallel to the ground – touching the outer knee with them in the middle of their length. This ensures lowering of silhouette and breaking it the in the hips and knees. Poles are positioned diagonally, causing a tilting of your shoulders away from the direction of skiing (counter-rotation), preventing the fairly common tendency to over-rotate one's torso to the direction of a turn. During the transition phase follow the L-H sequence and switch the body's position.

☆☆☆☆☆

AIM:

- torso counter-rotation
- low silhouette
- hip angulation
- L-H sequence

SKIING WITH POLES TUCKED UNDER KNEES

Make a long-radius turn, tucking poles under your knees. This position ensures lowering of your silhouette and weighting of the ski fronts (with hands at the back you have to lean forward to keep balance). You have only a limited ability to change torso's position, therefore precise skiing on the edges becomes all the more important. In the transition phase make an upward motion (as far as you can) and change edges.

AIM:

- **shoulders perpendicular to skiing direction**
- **low silhouette**
- **performing smooth turns**
- **weighting the tips**

CPSIA information can be obtained at www.ICGtesting.com
Printed in the USA
LVOW011431160113

315995LV00006B/8/P